How to be a Better Wife and Mother

Be a SuperMom, a Good Wife and Improve your Family Life Today

Amelia Farris

Amelia Farris

www.southshorepublications.com

© 2015 by SouthShore Publications & Distribution.

ISBN- 978-1514150252

ISBN-10: 1514150255

Amelia Farris

CONTENTS

Amelia Farris

1. INTRODUCTION

Sometimes it's natural to feel that maybe you aren't quite living up to your own expectations and being the perfect wife and mother for your family. Well, whatever is going on in your life right now, there is a solution. Things can and will improve. It is just a matter of finding the solution that works for you.

Let's just get one thing out of the way first of all, there is no perfection. There is only being the best you can be. Perfection is a television fantasy. There is only flow and function in life with yourself, your husband, and your children. Negativity will always exist; it's just a matter of pushing it out of the way and making room for the best aspects of family life.

Every woman is different. The way in which we do things and the way our families function differs from one person to the next. We may well share a lot of similarities, but at the end of the day, the very specific things that apply to each and every one of us are different in some way or another. So what works for one family, may not work for the next. Just think about your best friend and think about what is different between you and her. That is what is beautiful about us all, we are different.

This means that we can't judge ourselves by other people's standards. If you start looking at other people's lives and thinking how idyllic they are because of the way they run their home and the way their family functions, you will be fighting a losing battle. Appearances can be very deceiving anyway, there are underlying issues that cause friction in every family, no matter how well they hide it. What matters is how you deal with that friction.

The most important thing is that you create a life and a family that fits and suits you. If you only have an average household income, which isn't a whole lot these day compared to living expenses, this can cause many of the problems families face. You have to live within your means and enjoy the life and the luxuries that your income provides you. I promise you can feel like a millionaire at any income level if you just know how.

The fact that you are reading this and wanting to be better is a great step and shows maturity. We don't always know what to do intuitively and sometimes we need a little extra help and guidance. Admitting that and reading this book is a huge step in the right direction, because you have identified that there are issues that need solving and you are taking action to tackle them.

We also make a lot of mistakes throughout our lives and that just means that you're human. The most important thing is to learn from our mistakes. Also it is important to stop making the same ones over and over again.

I want to make something clear and that is getting better and being better is a never ending cycle. There are small things you never have to do deal with again, but every day is a new day and it's an opportunity to do the right things, or the wrong things. Essentially it's your choice in being better by making better decisions.

2. SIGNS YOU'RE DOING IT WRONG

There are certain specific behaviors that generally indicate that you're doing things wrong and going about things the wrong way. These are the main stumbling blocks that, in the long run, cause a lot of issues and grief for everyone involved.

When a person is single, certain actions are generally accepted, because the person is a bachelor or bachelorette and finding their way. When you are a mother or a wife however, there are certain things that you just can't do anymore. So let's take a look at what traits may cause someone to not be such a great mother and wife. If any of these apply to you then you will need to take action to remedy this issue as soon as possible.

A woman who drinks too much, drinks too often or is an alcoholic will generally make a very undesirable mother or wife. This woman is crying out for help. She has emotional issues that need to be addressed. A little professional help and AA can do wonders. There are a lot of places that help to get her life back on track. She has to want to of course.

A woman who swears and yells at her kids is not a very desirable wife and mother either. Kids will always pick up swearing at school from other kids, so let your home be a sanctuary where they can learn proper behavior. You don't want to be teaching your kids any bad habits. Only use standard words to describe whatever it is you're angry with. Shouting isn't a good way to teach children either. You may need to raise your voice sometimes but screaming at your kids and scaring them into doing what you want won't cause them to have any more respect for you. You should teach them discipline through clam and measured punishments instead.

A woman in a bad mood all the time is not a good sign. When a person has a mood problem there is almost always underlying issues and isn't just because they are a miserable person. Find out what is causing the mood, really think about what the issue is and try and figure out the best way of solving it. When you are happier, you family will be happier too and want to be around you more often and spend time with you.

A woman who takes no pride in her appearance or the cleanliness of her home is not setting her children a good example. Children learn by example. Their eyes are wide open to everything going on around them and they absorb everything that is happening. Being clean, tidy and presentable is something that children need to learn to get used to from an early age.

Flirting with other men either in front of your husband or behind his back, even if you don't act upon it, is extremely harmful. You don't have to be a saint. You want to be social but just watch the behavior don't be overly friendly with other men. People are always watching, listening, hearing, and remembering. Word can spread very quickly about things like this and get back to your kids or your husband. Even if they don't mention it, just hearing these kinds of rumors will have a deep and lasting effect on your family members.

Putting your husband down in front of other people or embarrassing him in public will cause a rift. This kind of behavior can cause distance in a relationship very quickly and it will show your children that you are not a team. Every man has faults just work with his positives and go from there. Try to put your past behind you and deal with the positive aspects of your relationship for the good of both of you.

Amelia Farris

3. BASIC STEPS TO BEING A BETTER WIFE

The first important step to being a better wife and mother is taking care of yourself. You can actually do this very effectively with a planned morning routine that you stick to every day. Some people will argue that they don't have enough time in the morning but there is. You just have to make time, even if it's by losing half an hours sleep and you need to go to bed half an hour earlier to make up for it. Taking care of yourself properly with a morning routine of course consists of hygiene, clothes, make-up and hair. Make a morning routine that enables you a time frame to do all of these things before taking care of anyone else. Taking this bit of time just for you will do wonders for your overall happiness and self-esteem.

Do what you have to do in order to feel happy. If money is tight, just find things within the limitations of your budget that make you feel good. You don't have to spend a lot of money, just simple things like making time to have a friend over for a tea and a chat a few days a week. When you feel good about yourself, it will rub off on your family and this will in turn enhance how good you feel even further.

Understand time and money. Help your husband by making the right decisions with the money you two have coming in. This is something a lot of women seem to find incredibly difficult. Find ways to be smart with time and money. If you two have a decent income then you can be making your way out of debt and you should start thinking about investing if you don't already. Don't be wasteful with money just because you are not the one going out and making the money. If you stay home and your husband works, be aware that he has had to go out and earn this money for your family. You should be appreciative that he does this for you and your children and not just spend it on things you want, especially if things are a bit tight at the moment. Even if you are wealthy enough to afford anything you want to, be smart with money. Your husband will notice this change, trust me. He will appreciate it more than you know.

Stop expecting your husband to be something he is not. If you think that another man is better than yours you may be right in some ways, but every man has flaws. You may see the outside of other people's lives and think they seem great, but they probably not as amazing as they look behind closed doors. The point is you need to make the best of what you have. Start accepting your husband for who he is. If he is looking for help then try your best to understand what he needs and give him a helping hand. If he is fine with himself, be fine with him. Make your life better because that usually is what it boils down to. It's your own reflection on him. By being happier yourself and being happy around him, he will be happier in turn.

Be sure your husband doesn't have unrealistic expectations of you. Things can go both ways. A man may have this perfect concept of what a woman should be like and you might be running around trying to live up to who he thinks you ought to be. This can create a lot of unwanted stress for both of you. Just make sure you know what your husband's vision is. If he is unrealistic let him know that he needs to get his head out of the clouds to come back down to earth. You two can discuss this and try to come to an agreement. People go through these phases in their life where they find themselves extremely unhappy with their partner, but this doesn't usually last forever. Sometimes you have to be strong and work through it together.

Schedule a date night with your husband. If you have kids and you don't want to get someone to look after them while you're out every week, just tell them to stay in their rooms and have a movie night with your husband. Most kids will do this anyway these days seeing as they have computers and video games to keep them happy. This will teach them that you two value each other as people, and give them a good example of how to treat their partners in the future. Even if they want to interrupt, just tell them that for one night a week this is how it's going to be. This teaches them how not to be selfish and also some discipline. When they know that they can't have everything they will be much healthier adults.

Amelia Farris

4. INTERMEDIATE STEPS TO BEING A BETTER WIFE

When you make mistakes, do you apologize? There are some people who just can't bring themselves to say sorry. My father was a classic example of one of these people. He would never admit he was wrong simply because he was too proud. This kind of behavior and mentality led to my parents getting a divorce. Since then he has worked on it and he has actually apologized to me personally for something he did a year ago, although I could tell it was very hard for him to do. The funny thing is, although it may have wounded his pride and made him think I lost respect for him for showing weakness and that he was wrong, in actual fact it made me respect him so much more than I did already for being big enough to admit it. Trust me, if he can change and start saying sorry when he is in the wrong, so can anyone else.

This relates to stubbornness and ego stroking. That's usually the root of not being able to say sorry even when you know you are in the wrong. Some people are just on a big ego/power trip and they feel like by backing down, even when they are wrong, they will be letting power slip. Well the sad truth is that people like this always end up alone in the end and the people around them won't stick about for any longer than they feel they need to.

All relationships, including the relationship you have with your husband should be balanced and fair on all levels. This is the only way you will maintain a happy marriage for both of you. Sadly, what this mainly comes down to is who seems like they care about the other person the least. The less you seem to care about the other person, the more power you have. This is extremely unhealthy behavior. You should both make it clear that you care about and appreciate each other often and tell them that you love them.

Ask for help if you need it. Run your household in an efficient manner, and if you realistically can't do it all, then don't be afraid to ask for help. A lot of women want to try to do it all. If you can simplify your life to be able to do that, that is fine. But there is no shame in asking for a little help here and there. When you have help, it helps you feel supported and less lonely. Don't try to do everything yourself just so you don't make any mistakes or whatnot. Just the fact that someone is helping out, even if they do make mistakes will make you feel better about your day to day tasks.

Watch the tone of your voice on certain things. Watch your tone of voice in general. If you haven't noticed, over time your voice might change as a result of stress or other reasons. You want to make sure that you are speaking to your husband as an adult. If you are disappointed, angry or stressed, all these things you can come across in your voice and cause stress for your family, which will then stress you out even more because they will be acting off with you. So make a point to control any unnecessary negative emotion in your voice when you are talking to your family members.

If you are holding on to resentment toward your husband. Think about all the things that have hurt you in the past and start writing them down in a journal. If they are stuck in your mind and you're letting these things dictate your actions, you must learn to let go of them. No one knows about them, or if they do, you might have been constantly talking about them and nobody wants to hear it anymore. If you're going to forgive and stay with him then you genuinely do need to forgive him. We all just want to be in the moment now. So let go of the past. Do some kind of significant action to let go, like crumpling the paper and throwing it away, or shredding it into tiny pieces. Let go of the past and live for the future. Think of yourself destroying the thing you wrote down every time you want to bring it back up and remember that you have made a commitment to yourself to let go of that resentment.

Smile as much as you can without being corny. A man loves a genuine smile from his lady. If he does not get it from you he will be searching for any woman to smile at him. Something as simple as woman's smile can have a big effect on a man. So try to smile more and make him feel good.

Be aware of your man's emotional state. Sometimes women think men are distant when they just don't want to be emotional. It is possible that something may be bothering him and he may want to talk about it or he may want to deal with it on his own. Just listen when he is ready to talk. Don't force him and know his body language and his facial expressions so that you are aware of what it is he wants when he needs it. Listen to him and take what he says as truth. Show your husband as much love and care as your kids. Don't let your husband think he takes second place to anyone.

Amelia Farris

5. BASIC STEPS TO BEING A BETER MOM

Praise your kids for the good things they do, don't always yell at them and give them attention for the things they do wrong. Do everything you can to build their self-esteem. One of the most important things in a person's life is to feel proud of who they are. You want to of course try to praise them for doing good things, so that their esteem is attached to accomplishment.

Smile at your kids. There have been many studies done into smiling and how it has an effect on those around you. Your kids will feel better and happier when you smile at them. They look to you as an emotional pillar. If you always complain or are angry then they will not be happy. They will absorb your way of thinking one way or another. They may not seem like they do now, but when they are struggling at any point in their life in the future they will remember how you handled stress. Just smile, it doesn't take much to make this change.

Be disciplinary, but also have fun with your kids. Don't always be telling them what not to do. Make sure you have plenty of time to plan fun things to do with your children. There is a time to learn, there is a time for activity for just the kids, but you always want to get involved and laugh with them. Play a game. Somehow be involved with your kids so they get a sense of you as a person not just as the person that tells them what to do. If you are happy, they will thrive off of your energy.

Read to your kids as much as you can while they are still young enough to want to hear stories. It doesn't matter what you are reading, but this is a great way to strengthen your bond with your children. Words lead to understanding, and the more words you can put in their head from birth to thirteen years old the better their minds will work for the rest of their lives. Read to them as much as you can.

You should constantly be reassuring your children and letting them know you love them. Even if they are getting a bit older and don't like the soppy stuff as much, you should still tell them you love them often. If children are used to you telling you that you love them every night before bed and saying it in return, this will stay with them into their adult lives. Some of my friends even tell their mother they love them at the end of every phone call, my family don't do this however. It's not the end of the world if you're not an overly affectionate family but if your children are still young, it's best to get them used to this behavior as it will make it easier for them to be open and express their emotions better as adults.

6. INTERMEDIATE STEPS TO BEING A BETTER MOM

Teach children at a very young age how to do things for themselves. Children are like sponges, and if you allow them to help you do certain small tasks that are safe, it will make things easier for you. More importantly it will also help your children take better care of themselves when they on their own. Things like helping to do the dishes and laundry. Younger children actually enjoy helping with things like this because it makes them feel like a grown up, so you will be killing three birds with one stone.

From day one with your children, mothers should stick to the very basics of cooking for most of the week. There are always special dinners and weekends for feeding kids other things that they like. It's your job as a parent to ensure your children are eating properly and healthily. You will be doing them no favors by giving in to their demands when they ask for unhealthy foods. Not only are you making them think they can get whatever they want when they want it and becoming spoiled in the process, but you are putting their health at risk. Vegetables are easy to dress and make taste good with butter, cheese, and herbs. When you have your kids eating healthy before they even know what healthy is, then they will just continue eating that same way into their adult lives. There is always time for cookies, cakes, and the junk food in moderation. Also keep portion sizes fairly small and kid sized.

On the flip side, take the kids out for ice cream once in a while. Let them have candy. Let them experience and try everything in the food department. When they get older, they will be familiar with a variety of foods. They will be able to make good choices, because they know what they do and don't like. Cook good, healthy food each day in general though.

Run your household a bit like a business. If you can try to get a rhythm and system down, then you will be able to master getting everything done in your house quickly and with time to spare. The purpose of this is so you can spend quality time with your family and also have time to just relax. When you feel on top of your responsibilities, you feel great. So work out a plan to get things done as quickly as possible each day and stick to it.

Control your emotions and don't let them control the way you act. Some women are very good at being practical and not very emotional, and others allow their emotions to rule their whole world. Emotions can ruin a woman's life if she lets them get out of hand so you need to be able to keep them firmly under your control. Emotions come and go. One of the reasons for the system in getting the house under control is because, no matter what you are feeling, if you have the system you are aware of what has to be done. The system allows you consistency. If you are not feeling so great, you still can accomplish your chores and then have a bubble bath and wine to de-stress later on.

Don't feel you have to hide so much from your husband and children, just be yourself and define yourself. Know who you are beyond being and a wife. If that is good enough then that is fine, but you still need to have your own identity. Find something you are good at. You can pick one thing to work on that is just for you. Defining who you are or doing something you are uniquely good at, keeps you from just doing everything for your family constantly and doing nothing for yourself. Knowing yourself helps you stand strong in something other than you motherly duties and wifely duties.

Amelia Farris

7. LIFE AS A GOOD WIFE AND MOM

So here is an example of what it is like to be a good wife. This woman's name is Mary. Now Mary is a manager in a department for a corporation. Nothing fancy but she works in an office building like so many other people. She makes an average living. She takes care of herself. She gets up every morning, follows her morning routine that sets her up for the day and puts on simple business attire. She eats healthily but nothing over the top. She feels confident in her abilities and herself. She likes the way she looks and she exercises in the morning, and goes for a walk every evening. Sometimes she manages to convince her husband to come and walk with her and they have a chat and catch up with each other's day. Other times she walks alone and has a chance to think about things and clear her head.

Mary works and makes her own money. She and her husband James both evenly pay into their mortgage. They talk about wanting certain things, so they make a decision to each have limits on a luxury item so they don't deny themselves anything. They make joint decisions on certain things, but then they have established certain things that they decide for themselves so they both still keep their individualities.

Mary did have a problem earlier in their marriage, because she didn't really agree with how much time James spent with his mother. She really wanted him home on the weekends to spend time together. They made an agreement that he would only visit with his mother every other weekend so they made a compromise, and things were much better between them as a result.

Mary makes a point to talk about things that James cares about. They have different interests, but they try to do something together outside of their home at least every other week. This way they are out together, away from the kids and are exposed to new things in life. They talk about the new things they see, and how they feel about what they did. Their drama scale is very low, and their life is peaceful.

Later in Life Mary gets pregnant and has a baby boy. The three of them are happy together, because they work together to try to make life great. They have their emotional flare ups as everyone does in a relationship from time to time, but they work on it together so everyone stays happy. They all support each other. Mary, her husband James, and their baby boy, Jason are a three person family unit. James does the laundry and Mary cooks the family meals. They both still work. Jason has to get to work earlier than Mary so she now brings Jason to day care. They rotate doing dishes every other night.

Mary shops once a week and cooking is not a big issue. She packs the fridge with vegetables, fruits, cheese, protein, and drinks like low sugar fruit juices and teas. She has kept giving her son different drinks until she has found ones that he likes that are also healthy. She keeps the fridge stocked up with the healthy foods that she has found he likes. She goes on the internet for ideas of what to cook. She keeps things very simple. Every couple of days she will make things a little more elaborate and spice things up. James will sometimes also cook just to help her out and give her a night off as cooking every day gets a bit tedious. Her main goal is feeding her family healthy foods. She also makes healthy pies, cakes, and cookies so when her guys want something sweet, they can eat it and she does not worry.

Mary reads to Jason every night after they have all brushed their teeth. She pays attention to subjects that make him happy, perk up, and ask questions. She talks with him as much as she can. He is not the biggest talker, and she understands this, but she makes sure that he is doing something he likes. He likes karate so she reads him books on karate and ninjas. He goes to karate class which also helps to keep him active and healthy. Jason is an only child so she makes sure she takes him to do activities where he can be in with other kids.

Jason knows that once a week he has to stay in his room and play games so that his mother and father can have their night together. He didn't like this at first but doesn't mind it anymore now that he is used to it. Mary likes to be good to her son but disciplines him when he steps out of line with fair punishments and doesn't lose her temper with him.

Mary makes sure she is on time for picking Jason up and getting him to where he needs to be. She tries to instill things in her son naturally so it is not so contrived, and she makes sure she doesn't force any one issue on her son. She knows that life is long for him and there is plenty of time for him to learn all of life's lessons.

Amelia Farris

8. CONCLUSION

Life is not a thought or one set way of doing things; it is a living, breathing, moving story that is in constant motion. It is difficult and it is fun. As a woman, there are demands put on us that we may or may not want to handle, but there is no use in making life more difficult than it needs to be by complaining and putting off the inevitable. When everything comes together, life is great and worth every moment.

The more you know, the better you can master your own life. It is important to be genuine and true. As a good wife and mother the simplest thing you can do is take care of yourself. This means make sure you eat, make sure you exercise. Your exercise can take 20 minutes a day, that's all. Many women live their lives healthily and only work on their bodies 20 minutes a day. Life itself is wear and tear on the body too so if you're constantly running about all of the time you may be getting enough exercise as it is. Your whole life in a day is enough to burn calories, if you need to, add a bit of exercise to this in order to stay fit and healthy. The fitter you are, the better you will feel both mentally and physically.

Remember be the best you can be. This does not mean you have to look like the women in the magazines because they get a lot of help from Photoshop. You have the ability to control what is going on in your life and inside your head. The rest you just have to maintain and participate in the best you can. You can't really control to much more than yourself, and you don't have to control other people. Just live your life as best as you can.

Just keep moving and solving problems little by little. Get the help you need to be the best you can and don't be afraid to ask for it. You can have just about everything you want just maybe not in the way you want it. Give yourself a little something special every week if you can. Thank other people for all that they do for you.

Your husband, if he is with you is a great man because he chose you over every other woman in the world. Help him always believe he has made the right choice. It's for the best for the both of you. Make changes if you have to and if that's what it takes to make him happier, as long as you're not sacrificing too much of yourself. Some things are not fixable but most are with just some simple changes.

So you should mainly just work on yourself and be better at being you. As you become happier, you will also get better at being a good wife and mother without even doing anything else. When you have put in the effort to go through your new routine of getting all the jobs done around the house, then you can sit back and relax at least once every day. You are entitled to this because you have earned it and because you know you are doing your best. This feels good and you deserve it.

Follow the advice and tips in this book, one step at a time. Try one of the tips today to get things moving in the right direction and get started on being a better you.

10. FINAL THOUGHTS

Well I think that about overs it for this book!

If you want to stay up to date with my regular free book promotions and to also find out about my future releases you can sign up to my mailing list at -
www.southshorepublications.com/ameliafarris

If you would also consider taking the time to leave me an honest review on this book on Amazon I would be extremely appreciative of your feedback.

You can find all of my other books, full of essential advice for women, by simply searching for "Amelia Farris" on Amazon.

Thanks for reading and I hopefully speak to you all in the next book!

CPSIA information can be obtained
at www.ICGtesting.com
Printed in the USA
LVHW021233080520
655241LV00012B/2216